DATE DUE

JUL 1 4 2010		
MAR 2 0 2012		
JUL 2 7 2012		

Demco, Inc. 38-293

What Are Things Made Of?

Text: **Núria Roca**

Illustrations: **Rosa M. Curto**

Look around you, and you'll see that the world is full of things! Some of these things come from **nature,** like the fruit you eat, but others are made by people, like your shoes.

People know how to make many things, but without nature we wouldn't know where to get the materials to make them**!**

Small babies drink **milk** from their mothers or from a bottle, and when they grow older they drink milk that comes from an animal with four legs and two small horns called... I'm sure you know it!

With milk, two awesome products
are made: cheese and yogurt!
Do you know any others that come
from milk?

Bees are very small animals with wings and black and yellow stripes on their bodies. They fly from one flower to the next and may sting you if you bother them. Bees live in beehives, where they produce **honey.** Mmmm, how sweet it is!

Cows give us milk, bees give us honey, and sheep give us... **wool!**

When winter is over, the sheepshearers, who are like barbers for the sheep, clip their wool very short.

With the wool they have shorn, people make yarn that may be dyed any color we want. Now the wool is ready to make sweaters and rugs!

Plants also provide us with lots of food, such as wheat to make bread, cocoa to make chocolate, or fruits for marmalades. But they don't give us only food. With flowers people can make ... perfume! And did you know that many, many medicines are made from plants**?**

Many different cereals are grown to make ...

Tea is a ...

Chocolate is made from ...

With fruit we can make …

From the sunflower we get …

Perfumes often smell like …

Some plants are used to make …

1   2   3   4

Have you ever seen **cotton** in a first-aid kit? It is so soft it looks like a cloud, but its threads were used to manufacture the fabric for your T-shirt. Even jeans are made out of it**!** Look how many cotton plants there are! With all this cotton we could make a lot of briefs and panties.

I'm sure you know a pencil is for writing (and you should not chew on it as if you were a mouse). But do you know what a pencil is made of?
With the **wood** from just one tree trunk we can make a lot of pencils, as well as toys, toothpicks, or houses. Of course, to build a house we need more than one tree trunk.

With wood we may also make notebooks for writing on or books like this one you have in your hands. It seems incredible, right? Wood is cut into tiny pieces, and then it is mashed until it looks like a soggy cereal called **paper paste.** The tissue handkerchiefs you use or the newspaper you read are also made from this paste. What else do you know that is made of paper**?**

We can get materials from animals, plants… and also from the **soil!**

We can remove **rocks** out of mountains to make bridges and houses.

Sometimes, we get so many rocks from a mountain it seems a giant took a big bite out of it!

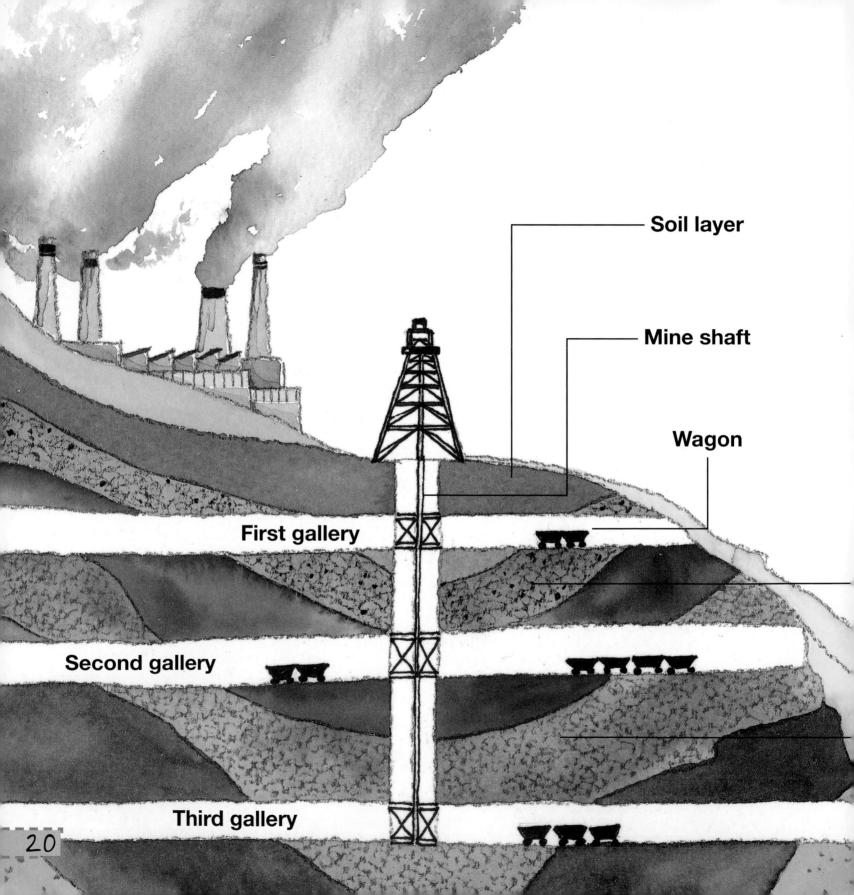

Soil layer

Mine shaft

Wagon

First gallery

Second gallery

Third gallery

20

Has your mom ever given you a sandwich wrapped in aluminum foil? Well, that aluminum comes from a **mineral** people find underground. This mineral is buried so deep down that people need to dig out tunnels to reach it. It is like looking for a hidden treasure!

Mineral-rich layers

There is a bad-smelling liquid that we buy for our cars at the gas station. Guess what it is**?**

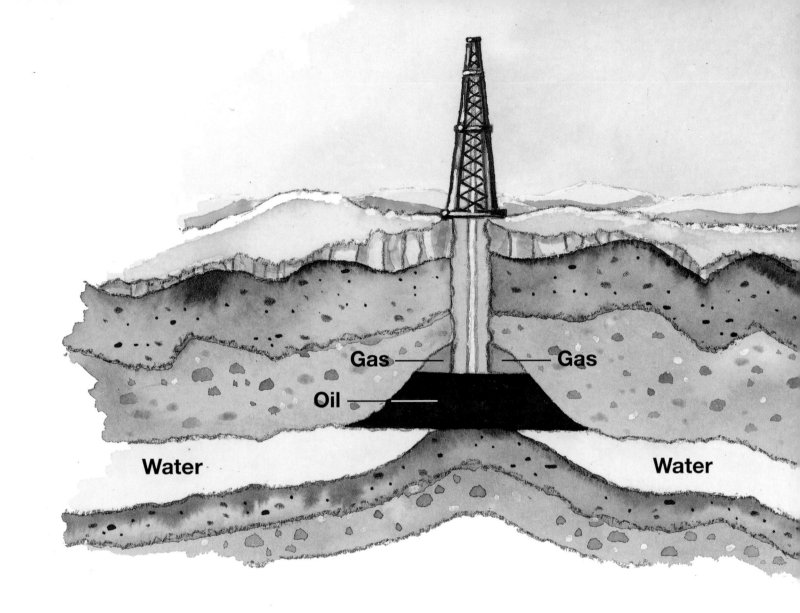

Gasoline is made out of **oil**, a liquid found underground.
Oil is also used to run the heating furnace in many houses
and even to make fuel for airplanes.

Yogurt containers, lunchboxes, toy trucks, DVD cases…they all have one thing in common: all are made of **plastic.** Plastic materials were invented by people: there are no plastic bags in nature…except those tossed around by careless people!

We use transparent **glass** for windows so light may pass through, for glasses so you may see what color your drink is, for train windows so you may watch all the places you pass by. What else is made of glass?
Don't hit it, because glass breaks very easily. And you may cut yourself badly with a piece of broken glass!

Find a button and look at it. What do you think? Is it a **material** made by nature or made by people? All around you there are materials that look and feel very different!

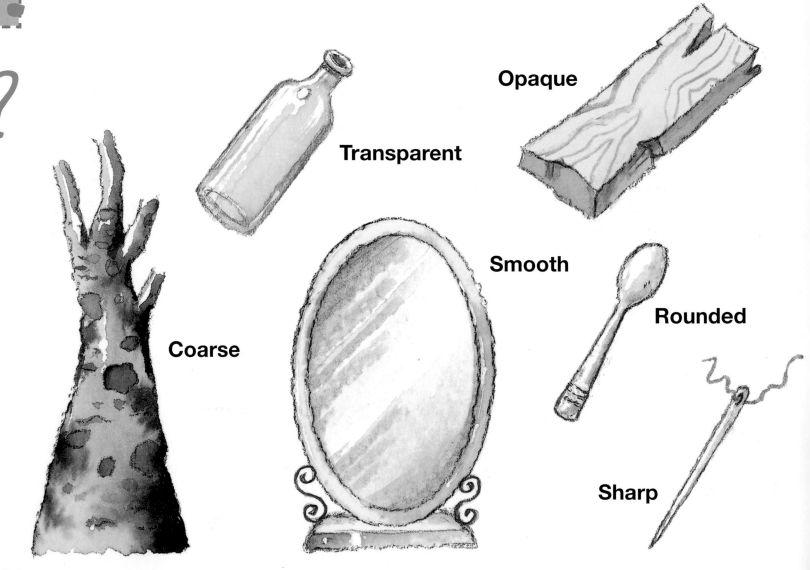

Opaque

Transparent

Smooth

Rounded

Coarse

Sharp

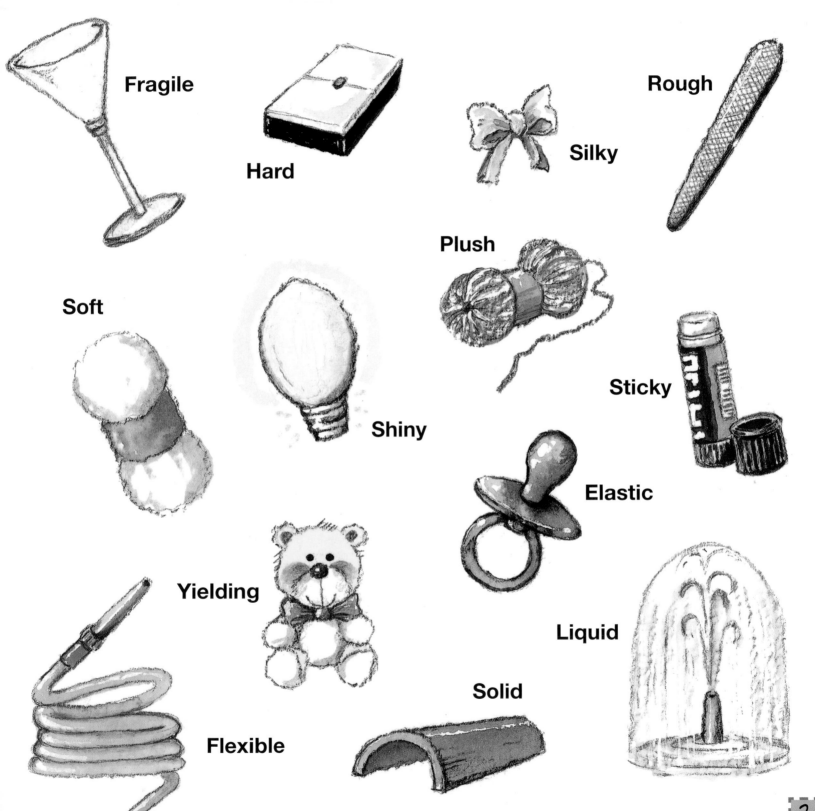

Fragile

Hard

Silky

Rough

Plush

Soft

Sticky

Shiny

Elastic

Yielding

Liquid

Solid

Flexible

29

Let's make marmalade

This is a very simple recipe to make marmalade. All you need is a grown-up to help you and the following ingredients:

- 2½ pounds very ripe strawberries
- 1½ pounds sugar
- 1 small lemon

Rinse the strawberries well and remove the stems. Once the strawberries are clean, pour the juice from the lemon all over them, add about one fourth of your sugar and let them sit. After half an hour, pass the fruit through a strainer and add the rest of the sugar. Put the mix in a pan and cook over low flame for about 20 minutes. Stir often. When the marmalade is cold, pour it into a clean glass jar. There, the marmalade for your toast is ready!

If you want the marmalade to keep for a long time, put the jar (uncapped) inside a pan with water and let the water boil for 15 minutes. Then, turn off the heat, put the cap back, and wait for the marmalade to get cold.

The marmalade is now ready for the shelf.

A homemade fabric

To make the clothes you are wearing, the fabric must be weaved first. Nowadays this is done in factories using huge machines, but before, all kinds of cloth were made by hand. Would you like to make some fabric?

1. Cut a square out of thick cardboard and make indentations at the top and at the bottom, as shown in the drawing. You may use thread or yarn to make the fabric.

2. Fix one end of the yarn to one of the top corners using adhesive tape, and then wind the yarn around the square, making it fit in the indentations at the top and at the bottom. The thread or yarn should be tight. After you have wound the yarn around all the indentations, thread its other end through a yarn needle.

3. To make the fabric, you need to pass the needle as shown in the drawing: first over one thread and then under the next. Repeat the operation until the whole square is covered.

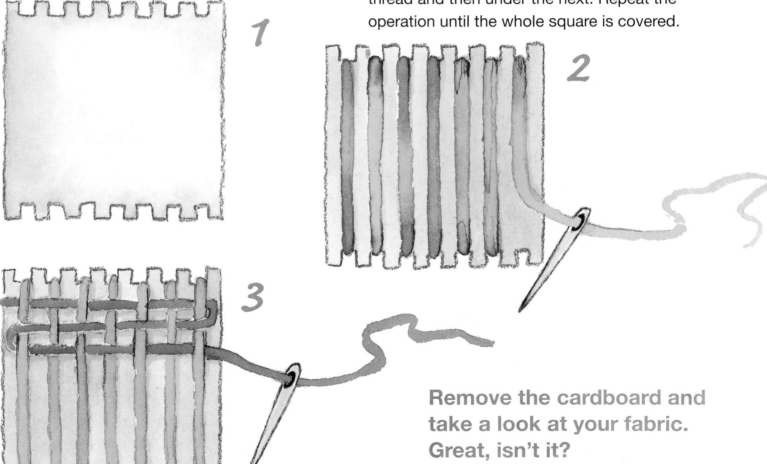

Remove the cardboard and take a look at your fabric. Great, isn't it?

Guess

You must say at least four true characteristics.

Collect as many buttons as you can. You may find them at home or ask your grandparents and even your aunts and uncles if they can let you have some. When you have a good number, put them all inside a shoebox. You may decorate the box gluing pieces of paper, threads of all colors, or any other decoration you like. Once the box is well decorated, you only need to cut a hole at the top, as shown in the drawing. Please notice that the hole has to be big enough for your hand to go through!

And now everything is ready to start playing with your friends. Take out all the buttons from the box and ask everyone to check them carefully. You may use a watch to know how long you may inspect them.

When time is up, put all the buttons back into the box. The first player is blindfolded and gets to put his or her hand inside the box and take out a button. The player has to say at least four characteristics about the button that are true. Here are some clues: How many holes does it have? Is it smooth or rough? Is it big or small? Is it round, elongated, or square? Is it made of plastic, metal, or wood? Do you remember what color it was?

Good luck!

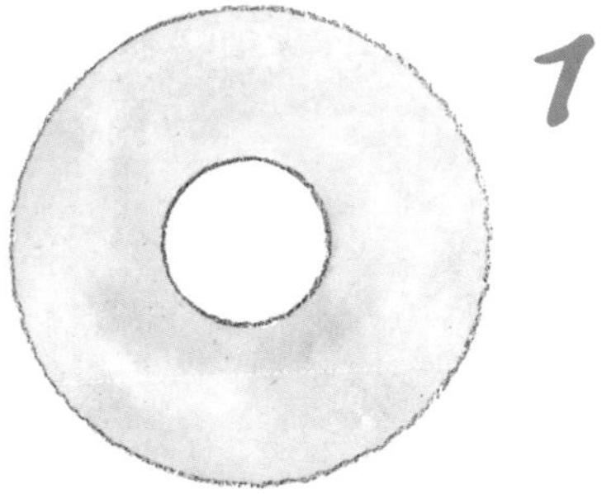

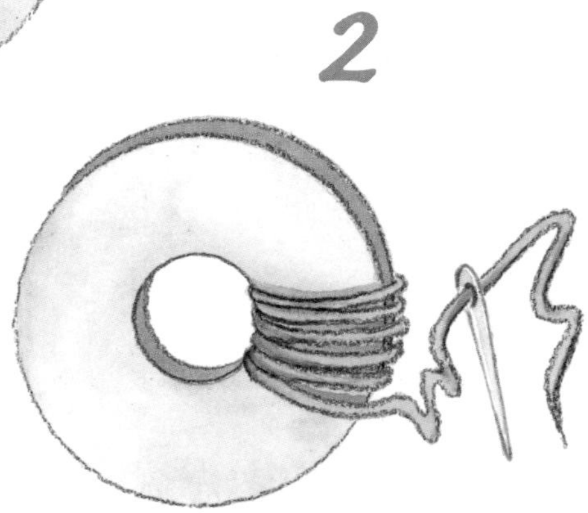

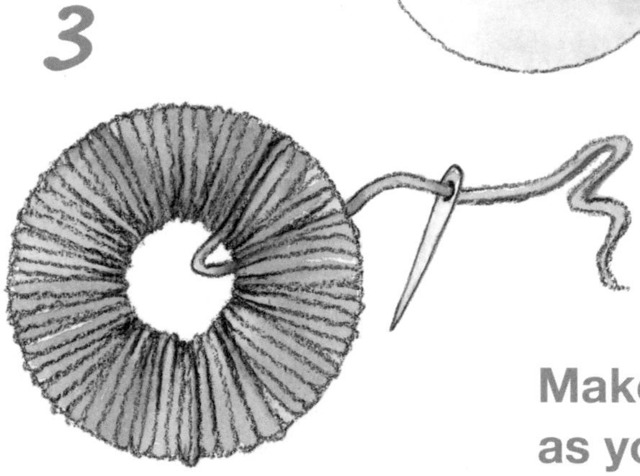

Woollen monsters

Would you like to make a woollen monster? You just need some yarn, a needle to thread yarn, and a piece of thin cardboard (the kind you find in a box of cereal). You will also need a grown-up to help you.

1. Draw two circles, one inside the other (like the ones shown here) and cut them out. You may make them any size you wish. For templates, you may use two glasses, one bigger than the other.

2. Cut a long piece of yarn, as long as the grown-up helping you is tall. You might need a chair to take the measure!

3. Make a loop with one end of the yarn around both circles and tie it. Then wind the yarn around the circles, but not too tight. Slide a thread behind all the yarn at the smaller circle, pull the thread to get all the yarn close, and tie it into a knot.

4. Cut the yarn along the large circle and remove the cardboard, and you now have a pom-pom. Use the rest of the cardboard for the eyes, feet, and tongue of the monster. Paint them, cut them out and glue them to the woollen pom-pom. Now you have a pom-pom monster!

Make as many as you want!

Note to parents

A world of materials

Primitive men had very few materials to work with. The first materials they used were stone, wood, bones, and animal horns. At present we have an enormous variety of materials. Some are natural, which means that we find them in nature, whereas others are man-made. Natural materials come from animals (wool, leather, fur, silk, horns, etc.), from plants (linen, cotton, wood, Indian rubber, etc.), or from minerals and rocks (stones, clay, gold, coal, oil, etc.). Parents should encourage their small children to observe different materials and to pay attention to characteristics such as color, size, shape, and the elements that form them. Children should also guess if these materials are found in nature or if they have been made by people. At this time, it is best not to talk about natural and artificial materials in too much detail, because children are not ready to grasp such concepts.

Honey

Bees suck a juice called nectar from flowers, and that's why we see them so busy flying from one flower to the next. With the nectar they make honey, which they store in their beehives. Depending on the flower where they get the nectar, honey has varying color and taste. Honey is very healthy, much more than sugar, but if we want it to keep its qualities, it is important not to warm it up.

Wood

To get wood we must fell a tree, cut up the tree trunk in planks, and let these dry slowly and carefully in the open air or in special dryers where warm air circulates between and around the planks.
In many places in the world, wood is obtained in a sustainable way, which means that not all the trees are felled but only a few. These are selected by a specialized technician who ensures that their removal will not affect the overall health of the forest.
It is important to find out the origin of the wood we buy, because all too frequently our wood products come from forests devastated by indiscriminate lumber operations. Let the little children know this, to make them aware that buying this kind of wood makes all of us responsible for the deforestation of our planet.

Paper

Paper is made from wood. The tree trunks are finely cut until they become wood shavings. These, in turn, are boiled in a chemical called caustic soda until they become a soft mass. This mass, which looks a little like papier-mâché, is subjected to a whitening process and then it is passed through a fine filter to separate it from its water contents. Finally, the mass drips onto a very fine moving grid, where it spreads and more water is removed. A number of hot

rollers press the soft mass, eliminating even more water and making it into a thin, smooth layer. Paper is used for writing, printing, wrapping, sanitary purposes, and making bank bills, post office stamps, posters, newspapers, books, and so forth.

Oil

Oil is used for heating and for running cars, trains, ships, and planes. We may also have heating by using natural gas, coal, or burning logs in a fireplace.

Oil is a liquid found underground. To draw it out, holes are made in the ground with a giant drill. Like all minerals, oil is found only in some places in our planet. This means that once it is extracted, it will have to be transported to all the places where it is needed. Oil may be transported by means of oil tankers, trucks, or huge pipelines.

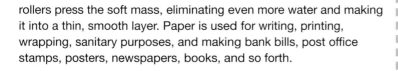

WHAT ARE THINGS MADE OF?

First edition for the United States and Canada
published in 2007 by Barron's Educational Series, Inc.
© Copyright 2006 by Gemser Publications, S.L.
C/Castell, 38; Teià (08329) Barcelona, Spain.
(World Rights)

Author: Núria Roca
Illustrator: Rosa M. Curto

All inquiries should be addressed to:
Barron's Educational Series, Inc.
250 Wireless Boulevard
Hauppauge, NY 11788
http://www.barronseduc.com

ISBN-13: 978-0-7641-3651-1
ISBN-10: 0-7641-3651-8
Library of Congress Control Number 2006931047

Printed in China
9 8 7 6 5 4 3 2 1